WINNING IN

HOSPITALITY:

FOOTFALL ON TAP

LEGAL NOTICES

"get rich scheme."

Your level of success in attaining the results claimed in our materials depends on the time you devote to the program, ideas and techniques mentioned your finances, knowledge and various skills. Since these factors differ according to individuals, we cannot guarantee your success or income level. Nor are we responsible for any of your actions.

Any and all forward-looking statements here or on any of our sales material are intended to express our opinion of earnings potential. Many factors will be important in determining your actual results and no guarantees are made that you will achieve results similar to ours or anybody else's, in fact no guarantees are made that you will achieve any results from our ideas and techniques in our material.

WINNING IN HOSPITALITY: FOOTFALL ON TAP

Proven methods to remove the guesswork when filling your hospitality business, stop wasting time & money on bad marketing & take back control of your business.

Dean M Sanders

WHEN THIS BOOK BEGINS TO RESONATE WITH YOU...

I'd be delighted to have a chat with you to discuss how to implement some of the marketing strategies contained in this book over a 'virtual' coffee.

My team & I can offer different levels of support to for your business needs. Perhaps you just need a quick chat to discuss your marketing plan & fill in some blanks. Perhaps you want us to build a couple of emails a week for you, schedule them & provide you with feedback on the results. We can do both and everything in-between.

Claim Your FREE marketing consultation by visiting...

www.hospitalityfootfall.co.uk

or scan this QR code:

Table Of Contents

INTRODUCTION

———— ◆◆◆ ————

This book will be about marketing and will be presented to you, on a silver platter, in three parts as follows.

Part one will cover the need for marketing, having the right mindset and establishing what you want to achieve.

Part two, perhaps the most important section (probably why you're here), will cover specific marketing tools or 'channels', how they can be utilised into 'mechanics' plus pros and cons and examples of each – your toolkit.

Part three will look at the way forward for your hospitality business and best practice on how to implement the strategies covered in part two.

You may get the most out of this book if you're a 'town centre mainstream young' (TCMY) business because that's where I've spent most of my career. However, I've also worked with Gastro Pub chains, Restaurants, Bowling Venues and many other businesses that rely on footfall to become successful – the price points and frequency of visits may be different along with the customer demographic, but the principles are the same. That's why this book is titled 'Hospitality Footfall on Tap' and not 'How to Fill Your Bar or Nightclub'.

In the hospitality trade, or industry if you prefer, marketing is referred to in a few different ways. You may call it 'bums on seats', filling your venue, pub or restaurant, engaging with your customers, advertising or even customer relationship management. I call it *Footfall* because in our venues what we need is Footfall above all else. If you run a restaurant you have a limited number of covers and in all other venues you have a capacity. First and foremost, you want to reach that capacity with a decent spend per head, then, when you've reached capacity, you want to increase the spend per head. Venues in the hospitality industry judge their performance on Footfall and spend per head.

Whatever terminology you use to describe your activity to get some or more Footfall into your venue and get them spending, what you're doing is marketing:

marketing

noun

1. the action or business of promoting and selling products or services, including market research and advertising.

Reading this book will make you look at your hospitality

business in a different way, without those rose-coloured glasses, without the sound of a crowd having a great time on a Saturday night, without the amazing aromas of your chef's latest mouth-watering menu additions and, most importantly, with zero ego or measuring of anything remotely masculine. Just a cold, hard look at the facts of your business. It could lead you to more or some success, it may convince you to change your path. That, reader, is up to you.

Through a series of my own experiences, I'll demonstrate some of the fundamental truths that I've learnt along the way (sometimes through huge mistakes) in thirty years at the sharp end of the hospitality industry. By 'the sharp end' I mean in the roles I've had from trainee manager through to a brief spell as an area manager, to a national Marketing Manager for a large pub group and on to being an owner, then Director of a hospitality Print Business and now as a specialist marketing consultant and facilitator to the trade.

We'll tackle in detail pros and cons of the specific marketing tools or 'channels' that you can add to your 'toolkit' of marketing skills. You'll learn how to use them practically and in doing so which ones suit your business, your style and your objectives. There will also be lots on what not to do! When we've looked at all of these, we'll put them together into a series of tried and tested 'marketing mechanics' – the stuff that works to drive footfall.

Ultimately, I'll leave you with a set of practical tools to reach your goals in the least painful way possible. After all, that's what we all want isn't it? To see the wood from the trees, know roughly what action to take and how to take that action. This book will be the opposite to the myriad of adverts on every social media platform that promise to grow your business by 200% just by watching a 3-minute video. Work is involved, real strategies that work will be added to your knowledge and implementing some of these into your business will increase your footfall over time.

In most hospitality businesses that I see if they just did the very basics right and spend ten minutes a day doing them right, footfall would never be an issue. I firmly believe that people thinking that this stuff is some kind of mystical dark art, that can only be done right by the gifted few prevents most people from even giving the basics a try, fact is - if I can do this most people can. Afterall, I started out as a glass collector. Sure, I've rubbed shoulders with marketing degree graduates, some were excellent at their jobs, some were utterly useless. I've been asked a number of times where I got my marketing degree – a question to be avoided in the corporate environment (if you don't have one) but that's never been an issue in my arena. Truth is, if I'd done a degree, I probably wouldn't know everything that I know now because I wouldn't have worked my way up through all of the jobs that I've done in hospitality. I may not also be able to effectively communicate with everyone in the industry as well as I do, from the cleaners to the CEO's.

SPOILER ALERT! This book was written during lockdown 3 in the UK during the Covid -19 worldwide pandemic. Footfall is bad right now.

So, there's the understatement of this decade and we're only one year in! But… if there's one thing that I've learned throughout my career it's that day follows night. That's to say good times will return for some of us, people will go out again, pubs, restaurants, bars and (even) nightclubs will reopen. When this will actually happen, we can't be certain of but we'll almost certainly get a bit of notice. To what extent people will return will depend on your target audience and perhaps where you are. When I was a Spring chicken in the (very) early nineties I remember asking an Operations Director of the large nightclub chain that I was working for as a Trainee Manager "how long do you think this recession will last and how bad will it be?" – his response has stayed with me. "In this industry we can be the first to be affected by a recession, but also the first to recover". Restrictions aside, this could be the same story again. There's a big BUT here… this time everyone will be opening up again at the same time vying for the business, it will be a great leveller and the operators that take action and don't just 'expect' things to return to how they used to be will prevail. We also don't know yet whether there's been, or will be enough of a break from the hospitality scene to change 'some' people's habits forever. We also don't know whether the new generation of Pub and Club goers, who have as yet NEVER been out, will do so. Take nothing for granted. A bit of a 'swagger' is always good in hospitality, if you really believe that your offering is fantastic it's a great start, but make sure that there's plenty of substance behind that belief.

Since those heady days of the early nineties, I've worked through three recessions, the massive deregulation of licensing laws, the smoking ban, one Millennium Eve and one Worldwide Pandemic. But let's try to focus on the positives.… Through moving with the times, in other words, continually learning and constantly being open to new ideas and a bit of grit and determination I'm still here, so you can be too.

A large part of my operational career was in nightclubs during the period when they were in serious decline, some would say that they still are, or were until they were all ordered to shut in March 2020. In 2005 there were 3144 nightclubs in the UK and by 2015 that number had dropped by nearly a half to just 1733. Indeed in 2008, the year my son was born, I bumped into an old operations director of mine and legend of the industry (sorry Tim, you're not old!). After swooning over how big my son's eyes were, he gave me a stark warning which I did take on board, but not straight away. "Get out of nightclubs" he said, and from his tone that I recognised from several 'talks' from years earlier I could tell that he was deadly serious. It was good advice unless you happened to be in a state-of-the-art, heavily invested 'big old boiler' in a city with two Universities. You'd also need to be experienced, happy to stay up until 5am at least 4 nights a week (therefore under 30 years old is good) killing it and/or very good at what you do with the luck of the Irish. I do know several people who fell into this bracket, most made their own luck by working hard, very few are left now by virtue of the fact that they aren't anywhere near under thirty anymore!

The reason that I tell you all of this is that very few of those criteria applied to venue that I managed around that time and subsequently, in my late thirties, I was still on a steep learning curve, battling for footfall.

Just to throw in some optimism though; a few years ago, I noticed that I was being asked several times a year how nightclubs were doing. People who asked me this were usually either fishing for a depressing disaster story, something that I've never facilitated, or waiting to pounce and suggest that I have a long overdue career change. My usual answer was to flip the question and say that the late-night industry was as strong as ever. Meaning that some types of venue – big old boilers in small towns, were not doing well and closing at a scary rate. But the same amount of people as ever were coming out to party and spending in the late-night economy. Not entirely true that but the demise of traditional 'night club' operations in smallish towns has happened several clear reasons that we can identify only some of which result in young people staying at home and not spending. Some of these, but certainly not exhaustive, are:

The Licensing Act of 2008: Put simply, this allowed any venue with a liquor license to stay open late, if they could make a case for it within the new law

The Smoking Ban: Smoking was still a thing when the ban came in forcing smokers outside. You could argue that it still is for the demographic who are likely to visit a nightclub.

The Drinking Habits of Millennials: It's widely accepted that Millennials are a healthier bunch, gym memberships have more than doubled in the past ten years and they simply drinks less.

Habits In General: Nightclubs have had a bad reputation of overcharging customers since before I can remember, the difference now is that customers have much more choice, not only in late night entertainment but in a plethora of other activities that they can chose from.

Whilst this book was written by someone who cut his teeth in nightclubs, nightclubs (I had to grudgingly admit some time ago now) aren't the be all and end all of hospitality or even the late-night industry. Far from it. So whilst many of the examples I give will feature nightclubs, the principles apply equally to any hospitality business. Fifteen years of my working life has been spent in various 'fights for business survival'. In times like that you learn a thing or two on how to survive and some interesting things about yourself.

A Cautionary Note Before We Continue…

Avoid breaking the law. Easy to say, and I've said it. Not so easy to do when your business is falling in around your ears and, if it's your own business, you're facing bankruptcy. If you're a manager you're facing redundancy, the destruction of a hard-won reputation and unemployment. I've faced both. I wouldn't say that I've deliberately set out to break the law when facing these situations but I may have been slightly blinkered and allowed some things to slide. At times it was made more difficult to 'avoid' by licensing laws being continually tightened, or at least that was the perception. At times big companies talk the talk but can leave you walking the tightrope as a designated Premises Supervisor and (relatively) easily replace you if things go South and you fall out of favour with the local licensing authority rep.

As well as the obvious licensing laws, you'll need to comply with Data Laws. We'll be looking in some detail at GDPR (General Data Protection Regulation) later in this book and I'll be explaining why, despite how you probably feel about it, it's actually a good thing and may actually save you money. In the meantime, you will need to register your business, in whatever form it exists, with the Information Commissioner's Office (ICO). This is because much of what we'll be looking at will be using customer data. In fact, if you employ staff you will already need to be ICO registered because you will be holding your staffs' details, whether this is on paper or inside a computer, so this is a heads up. For most ICO registration will cost just £40 a year and it will take you minutes to register online.

The bottom line is, if you're only way of increasing footfall is to flout the law, either get out now and choose another career or learn new stuff. On that note…

Shall we begin?

PART
ONE

Get busy & make your own success

Chapter One
TURN ON THE TAP

It's August 1990 and I've just got off the train from where I changed at Bristol Parkway. I have to say that right now, more than thirty years on, for the life of me I can't remember why I was so excited to leave Torquay in the middle of the Summer, all of my good mates and, in hindsight, the best time of my life. We worked hard (although it never felt like work) and we played hard. But I do remember that I WAS very excited.

Twenty minutes later I was sat outside a sunny fire exit helping to stuff 2,000 envelopes for the weekly birthday mailer. Surely this wasn't what I'd signed up for? Working during the daytime stuffing envelopes? Where's my new uniform and my new shiny gold badge? I'm not even going to go into detail about the branded shorts and T-shirt that I was forced to wear on my first weekend as a 'manager'. It felt like ritual humiliation, I was in Nightclub bootcamp. Mind you, my cohort for the branded 'throw-a-ball-through-a-hoop' competition looked better in the shorts than I did... silver linings.

When I had been accepted for the Rank Leisure Management Trainee programme I was absolutely delighted, I also had absolutely no idea what would be involved. On day one I learned my very first lesson. You don't just open the doors and let the people flood in, you need to work at that. Especially if it's a small town with two big nightclubs and, apart from on pay weekends, there aren't enough punters to go around.

Work on it we did. There were weekly direct mail shots, Birthday mailers, regular weekend promotions, tens of thousands of flyers printed and distributed with different types of incentives and offers. I was introduced to the 'contrived let' – good old-fashioned word of mouth did the rest and we killed it.

Our main opposition nightclub, also just over a thousand capacity, was just up the road and around the corner was brand new with state-of-the-art sound and light, a good DJ and similar promotions and offers. But they were stone dead. We did that. Or more accurately the talented and entrepreneurial General Manager who was my boss did that. In this instance, that was the difference between our success and their failure…. Relentless effort.

Of course, there were a few other elements to our success. We looked after the venue, everything worked and if something broke it was fixed. Even though it wasn't brand new like our competition, it had a good layout – central dancefloor with a 'circuit' for cruising around. Our staff had good moral, we looked after them and put the right characters in the right jobs. We looked after our customers and had zero tolerance policies on violence and drugs and backed this up with a well-oiled machine that was the security team and we all read from the same hymn sheet looking after one-another.

Because of all of this, though I probably still didn't realise it and was still, for the most part, just having a good time, the management team of 1990 at Newport Ritzy all achieved their individual objectives, together as a unit – even if some were clueless that there even was an objective. First and foremost, we got to keep our jobs. Margaret Thatcher was still Prime Minister of the UK and I was learning fast that there were no 'free rides' in the real world. The General Manager moved to a bigger, twin-scene venue in a City with, no doubt, a bigger salary. The Deputy manager moved to an equally exciting new challenge. And the green-behind-the-ears-trainee slowly became a lighter shade of green, dropped the 'trainee' in his title and moved to an interesting spell at a three-thousand capacity venue in Bristol which included a two thousand capacity nightclub, bars and a banqueting suite.

I have a hundred stories (well at least fifteen) about my time as a trainee nightclub manager, most aren't relevant to this book but may appear at some point on social media. One that does stand out is and should have been a very simple but effective message for me when I was just 21 years old. One day the area manager came to visit. One of most switched-on operations managers that I've ever met who just oozed knowledge and experience. He took me aside and asked me a very simple question: "Dean", he said "What are we doing here?"

It wasn't designed as a trick question. I said a few things… "Well, we're serving customers drinks and giving them a good night, aren't we?" "We control the door, keep the bar stocked and do weekly stock takes". "We send out mailers every week" I hadn't missed the point because I had no idea what his point was and he knew it.

"We're here to make money" he said, "and everything else, however enjoyable it may be, is a toward that goal."

I was very much in a corporate environment back then, but that's one thing that they always get right in a corporation; it's all about the profit. Even if that isn't the main reason that you're doing what you're doing, which is, of course, very common in our industry – it's a passion. It's very important to remember that fact in everything we do, not least, because if we don't, we won't be doing the things that we enjoy doing for very long! In the hospitality industry it's easy to get caught up in the subjective and lose sight of the objective. Be honest, how often have you lost sight of this whilst in the middle of your daily routine? And how often have you chosen a type of marketing activity based on how comfortable you are in doing it rather than what you perhaps know may work better with a bit more effort? You're not alone so don't beat yourself up too much.

Much is said about 'mindfulness' these days:

mindfulness

noun

the quality or state of being conscious or
aware of something.

Hopefully you're as 'mindfully' reading this book as I am writing it! How many times so far has your mind wandered off into something as you were triggered either by your own imagination or by something that you've read, or both! Did you realise that you hadn't actually read the previous half a page and if so, did you go back and read it again so that you took in what was on that half page? It's a choice.

The point is that I want you to act with purpose and be mindful of that purpose and how it supports your objectives. It is no longer, and hasn't been for a long time, good enough to simply exist as a hospitality business. Market forces will not allow it. You could be in the best location of the busiest area of a major city, but if you don't get your offer right the competition will take them from you. Even if you're still busy it won't be enough to pay your large rent to be in that location.

Put in another way, this is not 'Field of Dreams' – if you build it, they will NOT come'!

After my position was made redundant from one nightclub in 2009, I was asked to help with the opening marketing of another in the same town just days later. We cleaned up on the opening weekend, partly because of the job I did – at the time a new platform that you may have heard of, 'Facebook', was very popular with the nightclub-aged demographic (not any more). We also had some big PA's which came with a big price tag. Week two was also huge but in week three numbers started to decline and some cold hard truths emerged. More on those later!

The owner that I worked for asked me soon after the end of week four, "Are there not enough customers to go around?" I was a bit surprised to say the least at his question. "No", I replied in matter-of-fact fashion, "we need to steal them". This was obvious to me for a few reasons. The biggest reason was that prior to this new club opening I had been running a club down the road where we had operated for the previous two years without the new venue. We had done quite well, reaching capacity on most Saturday nights, but we weren't turning away a thousand customers on a Saturday night because we were full at 11:30pm! Those days were long gone, never to return.

So, before we continue, let's decide that we are going to increase the footfall in your venue. We're going to decide how much business we want; we're going to set realistic goals and we're going to implement a mindful strategy to achieve those goals. We're deciding to turn on the tap because we need more footfall and it's not going to happen on its own. Furthermore, we're going to decide where those customers are, target them and steal them from your competition where necessary. Look, I'm not suggesting we use underhand tactics, although many would, I'm just saying that they are fair game and have the freedom of choice. Of course, much of marketing includes positioning too and if you think that your competition has already unassailably cornered the market in a particular area, go for a different one - reposition yourself.

Chapter Two
FINDING YOUR BASE BUSINESS

———— ✦ ◦◆◦ ✦ ————

H aving laboured the point that people won't flood into your business on their own without you taking action, let's look at what your 'base business' is. That's the amount of business that you do week in, week out without the new marketing toolkit that I'm going to share with you. Your business is most likely both seasonal and cyclical and there will be other natural peaks and troughs too as well as key dates in the calendar.

SEASONAL trends: If you are a restaurant in a southern seaside town, you'll be busier in the summer months as the tourists arrive and quieter in the Winter when they are few and far between.

Example of a CYCLICAL trend: Simple – pay weekend, unless you're in a very good or very bad seasonal trend, you'll see an uplift in your business on a payday weekend every month to some degree.

Examples of KEY DATES: The obvious ones out of Christmas that could be defined as 'seasonal' are Valentine's Day, Mothers' Day and Fathers' Day for Restaurants and Gastro Pubs. A Level results Day for Nightclubs and Bank Holiday Weekends for most hospitality businesses, unless you're a Pub in the heart of a City Business District.

You should have a pretty good idea of what this base business is and if you haven't it's a very good idea to spend a little time finding out by looking back over your records for at least a year if you have them. If you can look back two years and eliminate any outside influences that will tarnish your peaks and troughs – lockdown from a global pandemic is the obvious one. In truth we're sort of starting again after that one aren't we? You can look back and see what you would expect to do next summer from what you did a couple of years ago. But, as I mentioned earlier, how may trends change as a result of the lockdown? Nobody really knows exactly and for everyone that accurately predicts it, there will be somebody that got it completely wrong. What's clear though is that now more than ever, we are responsible for how well we all bounce back. Let's do everything in our power to try to achieve that, and give ourselves the best possible chance of manifesting that reality.

I'm a big believer in cosmic ordering. But wait, before you get an image in your head of me dressed in purple suede shoes hugging tree, please hear me out…

For me it's all about mindset and DECIDING to do something. Put simply, if you believe in something, want it to happen and, most importantly, you can see a clear framework of how it can be achieved that isn't like rocket science to you – then you've taken a huge step to making that thing a reality just by deciding in your head to do it. You'll find that your mind is working to solve the problems that stand in your way even when you're sleeping and things will start to happen.

But enough woo woo. Another way of describing your base business is 'where you are now', albeit a more thought-out accurate way of saying it.

Next, we need to know what you aspire to. Think big. There is a saying that goes:

"It's a fact that people who aspire to nothing hit their target with remarkable accuracy 100% of the time".

So, the sky shouldn't be a limit here. Sure, you'll need to be realistic when we look at timescales, but for the moment we're thinking more globally. So, what's the bigger picture of where you want to be in, say, two years' time? If you have thought REALLY big, then break that down into achievable steps, after all you may need another venue to make your big dreams a reality and we're not looking at that today, we're looking at increasing footfall in the venue you already manage. But hey, prove a winning formula here and the sky really is the limit, right? Shoot for the moon and if you miss, you'll hit the stars...

So, now that you know your base business and where you want to be (thinking big, not just breakeven) you also know how much extra business you need. Furthermore, as we mentioned at the start of this book, you know what your average customer spend per head is. So, know you know how much extra footfall you need to reach your target. Now let's decide when that footfall needs to happen.

Above and Below the Line

So, having NOT done a marketing degree and for half of my career (at least) not known that I was in marketing, I was oblivious to the terms widely used by 'clever' marketing people: 'Above the line' and 'Below the line'.

'Above the line' marketing activities are aimed at a mass audience usually for brand awareness rather than a specific call to action. Media such as TV, radio, newspapers, magazines and bus advertisements all fall into this category. SME's in the hospitality industry rarely carryout ATL marketing activities these days. Going back nearly twenty years, local radio advertising was a useful media for a decent sized nightclub in a small town, but even then, we didn't really know what return on investment (ROI) we were getting and we didn't even try to find out what it was. We seemed to be just throwing a lot of mud at the wall and if we were at capacity on Friday and

Saturday nights, above target and within marketing budget, everyone was happy. If we weren't, the budget would drop and the activity would stop – at the time when we should probably have done more advertising!

All of the strategies that I'll be discussing in this book are 'below the line' (BLT) activities, much more targeted and targeted at smaller groups. Therefore, these activities are more measurable and, depending on what the mix is, less costly. They may, however, require more planning and management but you will be able to focus your efforts on what works.

One of the reasons that BTL marketing is the obvious choice is that we will need to target specific groups for both different offers and different days of the week. The classic example of this is nightclubs with student focussed nights and nights focussed on town residents. Usually, the two don't mix but are both important markets. Another example in a different operation could be a gastro pub operation that serves a traditional Sunday Roast. Their typical customer for that is probably very different from people visiting after work for a drink with colleagues on a Friday evening. There will be some crossover, but it's important to be aware of the different demographic.

A breakdown of your current business

So now begin to look at your business in detail and break this down into sessions. If you're open 7 days a week, for example, from 11am until midnight, then I suggest breaking this down into fourteen daytime and evening sessions. This may all seem very obvious and you may already know, or have a very good idea of what business you're doing on every one of those sessions, but this is a useful activity for a few reasons…

I'm willing to bet that there may be one or two surprises when you look at the figures in detail:

This could be on a session or sessions that you're not normally at your venue when it's open. Here's a hypothetical scenario (but close to things that I've experienced): You always take a Tuesday off and everyone at your Gastro Pub knows it. You've known for two years that revenue on Tuesdays are not good, about the same as Mondays, but you see Mondays because you're in doing stock takes and other paperwork. Tuesdays have been sliding a bit more in the past six months, but you're only seeing the full day picture and your assistant Manager, who cashes up at the end of the night, just reports a slow evening.

When you look at the day as two sessions you see that, in fact, all of the recent drop in revenue is from the daytime session. You ask your assistant Manager if they can offer any insight. They tell you that they started to close the kitchen half an hour early on a Tuesday every week because the chef needed to do the school run every Tuesday afternoon and it's really quiet anyway.

You look at the session figures since this started and see a slow but consistent gradual decline in revenue on Tuesday daytimes. People have learned that you close early on Tuesdays and have gradually stopped coming.

You will see the real picture:

If you base your knowledge and therefore make strategic decisions about your business based on either your perception of the business or what others are telling you about your business rather than what the session figures show, then you may not be seeing a true picture. Your decisions could be fundamentally flawed and you could be heading in the wrong direction.

You have a starting point from which to measure the successes of your marketing:

You'll see exactly where your efforts have made an impact and crucially, you can replicate the things that work. Someone (not me) once said "Half of the money that you ever spend on marketing is wasted – the real job of a marketing manager is to find out which half". The same can be said of the effort that you put into your marketing. Time is money.

You'll start to see where the best opportunities are:

Ten years ago, I was the GM of a fifteen hundred capacity seaside resort nightclub that traded only three nights a week.

Friday, Saturday and Sunday. This wasn't too bad at the time but we were, of course, constantly pushing for more. There were, at that time, two main competition venues with a similar style of operation. One of these was two-hundred yards away, only opened on Friday and Saturday nights and was widely recognised as being for the more 'discerning' club goer. Everyone is more discerning these days, more on that later.

The other competition venue was a mile and a half away on the other side of town and open on Thursday, Friday and Saturday nights. Their Fridays and Saturdays were decidedly average, nowhere near capacity but with an 'ok' atmosphere. Their Thursdays, on the other hand, were huge and had been for as long as anyone could remember - probably about 3 years! (Which is an eternity in nightclubs).

I bumped into the GM of this venue one night. We shared a friendly rivalry; he was quite an experienced manager for whom I had a degree of respect. He, on the other hand, may have underestimated me somewhat. We chewed the fat on the state of clubbing in the town, we all needed more business, as ever. He suggested that I should go after the trade of a 'late bar' that was doing quite well on a Wednesday night and was very close to me. I quipped that I was "much more likely to go after your Thursday night". "Good luck with that", he replied, "you'll never get my Thursday customers."

Hmmm... Well, being a red-blooded male and having come from an environment where having a competitive nature was pretty much drummed into me for the first five years of my career, I embraced this challenge. For me there's nothing like being told that I can't do something (i.e., I'm incapable of doing it) to motivate me to actually get on and do it.

I decided to put in a series of relatively inexpensive promotional activities in a six-week run of Thursday nights with sensible drinks pricing and content to hang our hats on. By content, I really mean 'something to promote'. This is quite an interesting thing to note and something that you'll need to think about as a key part of your marketing plan. More on this later too.

So, we put in place a couple of foam parties three weeks apart, a band member DJ set, an inexpensive Public Appearance (PA), an 'Old School' night and a 'Traffic Light Party'. I'm not suggesting that if you're in the TCMY market these are your 'go to' list of promotional activity. Things have moved on a bit in the last ten years and customers have become more discerning, did I mention that before?!

So, we hit it hard and six weeks later we had a storming Thursday night which we had stolen from the competition, job DONE! Err, well, actually no we didn't. We managed to get a few hundred each week and a relatively 'OK' atmosphere which, sadly, wasn't sustainable long-term.

So why am I telling the story of a failed attempt to get a new Thursday night off the ground you ask….? Well, because something funny happened on the way to the Moon. Remember when I said earlier, "shoot for the moon and if you miss, you'll hit the stars"? In this case the 'star' we hit was literally shutting down the competition. It turns out that around 60% of their Thursday night crowd were deeply loyal but the other 40% came to our new Thursday night. This meant that over the course of six weeks, lost their atmosphere and along with it their reputation for being a solid bet for a great night out on a Thursday. As this Thursday night session was propping up the rest of their business (they were already not very busy at the weekend), within a month the owners had decided to throw in the towel and closed the venue.

The manager was right, in some respects: even with their closure, we didn't ever get their Thursday crowd, we had already stopped our Thursday nights before their closure. But we now had a share of their Friday and Saturday night customers, which more than made up for it. Plus, there was no longer a Thursday night in the town, so those customers spread out to the other nights too.

There were several things going on here:

People are creatures of habit.

Our job when we're marketing in hospitality is to change those habits and when we do, customers will likely stay with us until someone else comes along and tries to break the new habit that we've created. It was no fluke that we went for a six-week run of promotions, we knew that if we could break those habits for six weeks, we would change them.

People go where people are.

These days we talk a lot about 'social endorsement' being a very strong motivator for people to make a purchase and companies invest huge amounts of money into driving reviews on platforms like Trustpilot and obviously different social media platform also. Truth is, people have always voted with their feet and this is never more important than when 'footfall' is your venue's primary measure of success. One of the things that our industry is always up against is how quickly we create atmosphere. Even when you're out for a meal with your loved one in an intimate setting, NOBODY wants to be the only couple in an empty restaurant. If you've ever taken your significant other to an environment like this, you'll know what I mean. You can't help the underlying feeling of "what's wrong with this place? Why is it so quiet? I've made a mistake, the food must be awful, or there's somewhere much better down the road where everyone else is and we're missing out on that"!

TCMY venues and in particular late-night venues have always battled with this and nightclubs found it extremely difficult to cope with the effects of the 2007 de-regulation of licensing laws allowing pubs and bars to open after 11pm. All of a sudden, they didn't have queues of people desperate to get in anymore. Door charges started to become frowned upon, customers had more choice and large capacity venues in smaller towns started to suffer badly.

People can be fickle.

Never overestimate your market position, as a shiny new venue, or an operator with passion and drive can ruin your party in a relatively short space of time.

Be aware of what the competition are doing.

Don't overdo this and spend too much time out of your business, but you need to be aware of what's happening in your market or you won't be able to adopt appropriate countermeasures.

Take a strategically planned course of action and you'll begin to get 'lucky'.

I said earlier that some of my pier group of managers made their own luck. This was in the main by taking a considered and *mindful* or 'joined up' approach to their marketing. They would be able to tell you exactly what they were doing at any given point in time, and what's more, why they were doing it.

Half of the time they made it look easy and fun and for them it would be as easy as shooting fish in a barrel. They knew that they would prevail because they knew that their competition wouldn't take the necessary action to defend their businesses. This was either because of a lack of experience and knowledge, few resources or just plain laziness on their part.

PART TWO

Your Hospitality Marketing Toolkit

Chapter Three
MARKETING TOOLKIT: WHY YOU NEED TO COLLECT DATA

W hen my career in hospitality management first began most businesses didn't use computers on a daily basis.

That statement seems alien to most of us now, especially to anyone born after 1980 who would have been taught the new subject of 'IT' from the start of secondary school. When I was at school, we had use of a couple of 'BBC' computers in a small cupboard in the sixth-form, but that was IT!

So, in 1990 we relied upon the electoral role, very useful back then but not much use and outdated today, plus our own typed-out database. We would type names and addresses onto A4 paper so that we could photocopy them onto envelope labels which meant that they would be in date-of-birth order. This would allow us to send our birthday mailers every week like clockwork. Well, usually the job wall fall to us junior managers, the DJ (whose job back then also included promotions at no extra charge), and the odd member of staff who may have popped in to pick up a jacket that they had left behind after work on Saturday night. It was DULL, we didn't really want to get stuck doing it every week for hours on end and some of us didn't see the point as we were clueless of the bigger picture. The fact is that we relied heavily on the weekly mailout, it had to hit at just the right time, not too early that the potential customer hadn't started thinking about their birthday plans yet and not too late so that had already planned to go to the competition. So, it was vital that the mailer went out on time, not least because if it was late, we'd have to send it first class – the cardinal Sin. Hence the shout would go out on a Tuesday afternoon: "Get that bloody mailout OUT!" Life, it seems was so simple back then.

Where Data collection is concerned it's bit like the old saying: "It's easier to go downhill than up, but the view is from the top." It is much easier not to collect Customer Data but if you do it and do it well, then you will have a serious advantage over your competition, who, in my experience are probably not doing it. It never ceases to amaze me that most hospitality businesses don't collect their customers' Data, especially these days when the process can be automated to a massive degree.

One of the reasons why they don't collect Data is because they have fallen into what I call the 'Social Media' trap. All of their marketing is done on Social Media so in their minds they don't need to collect data, it's already there on their Social Media platforms. Let me clue you in on why this is a huge mistake.

Social Media platforms move the goalposts to suit them every five minutes.

Remember when you could post on Social Media and all of your friends or likes would see the post – that's ancient history. These days, as you probably know, you need to spend real money out of your marketing budget to 'reach' your audience, basically in a bidding war with your competition. Not only this but the structure of the platforms can change and not always for the better, buttons disappear and the way you've done your marketing in the past may not be possible going forwards. The bottom line is, you have no control over that, no certainty. Businesses need certainty, or at least as much control as possible.

Everyone else is doing exactly the same thing.

It can quite effective as part of your marketing mix but do bear in mind that all of your competitors will be doing the same.

You don't own the data!

If you lose your login details, an old member of staff locks you out of the account or you get banned for a dodgy post; then your likes just disappear. You don't have them stored in the cloud to print off or upload. They're gone. You start again.

Don't get me wrong, you need a social media presence on the platforms that are appropriate for your demographics, almost as much as you need a website, and they can be a decent part of your data-capture automation. Check-ins are pure gold and reviews are a must for that all-important source of social endorsement that we discussed earlier. But you need to mix it up a little and don't rely on SM for too big a chunk of your marketing, because when those goalposts move, so will your customers.

So that's why I'm not going to cover Social Media marketing in this book, at least not in detail, just in the context of its place in some marketing mechanics covered in Part Three later. I am an expert in Social Media (just like the rest of the World) and I am a fan, to a point, but the opportunities for increasing your footfall don't lie in doing exactly the same as everyone else, or in what you're already doing, it requires a more mindful approach...

It takes effort to take a U-turn from the social media trap, but the sooner you start, the better. When you do, you'll be taking control of your marketing by building a list of your customers and *potential* customers. You'll be able to control what these people see and when they see it. You'll be able to segment your customers' data allowing you to target them with pinpoint accuracy.

If your business is flying right now it's even more important to collect Data whilst footfall is good. Your customers are more likely to give you their Data when you're popular, because there's more of them, obviously and because, well, you're popular! You can then save this for a rainy day, when you're not so full and you need a boost.

But for a few exceptions that I've encountered in the past thirty years, hospitality venues are cyclical. When a brand-new venue opens, if done right, it's popular. Eighteen months down the line when it's not so new and a newer venue has opened up the road, it's not as popular and eventually, certainly within four years, you will need to reinvent yourself to gain popularity again. A reinvention requires a serious investment and many 'Independents' will falter at this stage of the business lifecycle. If you have a large strong customer database, you have the tools to increase the lifespan of your venue as part of a proper planned marketing approach, rather than a desperate bid to stay afloat.

Most of the companies that I've worked with understand the need to drive Data collection and the amount of data that they collect is a key performance indicator for their businesses, especially for the clients that operate multiple venues. For example, one of my customers is a business that grew, within a ten year period, from one to thirty-five venues. Each venue, as it opened, used my platform to drive data from the start. 'The

Footfall Driver' is an online suite of digital marketing tools centred around a sophisticated database. As every venue is using the platform it's easy to create a spreadsheet of KPI's that show which venues are most active in collecting data, how many text and email messages they are sending out and what sort of open rates they are getting. In every case the level of proactivity of the management team in collecting data correlates directly with the success of the venue. Managers that actively collect data also do more proactive marketing campaigns and have more successful venues. Of course, these managers are also more proactive in every area of their business, but you get the idea.

Sometimes managers can show unwillingness to embrace Data collection and digital marketing. Usually this is because they are in the 'Social Media trap', sometimes they are a little over confident, sometimes it's seen as a short-term solution to saving a little money during a dry spell in the business which is a very bad idea. At a meeting of senior operational staff, a couple of years ago, the Managing Director of that company, a big fan of the Footfall Driver famously said, "If a manager isn't using the Footfall Driver, don't get rid of the Footfall Driver, get rid of the manager".

Chapter Four
MARKETİNG TOOLKİT: GOOD DATA

———————— ✦ ▸◆◂ ✦ ————————

Good data is good, bad data is bad. A bit of an over-generalisation there and pretty obvious too but let me define both to explain in more detail.

In a nutshell good data is data that will be in your database because it has been collected in one of the following ways:

Your contact has filled in a form either online or in the old-fashioned way on a flyer. They have done this because they are interested in receiving information from you. This could be details about your opening or a specific offer even a competition entry. Furthermore, they have ticked a box to 'opt-in' to receiving communications.

The contact has made a booking with you and used their contact details to confirm that booking.

They are a customer and have logged into your customer WiFi using their details and opted in to receive communications.

You have bought a data list from a data supplier with an

audit trail for where the data was attained by that supplier. You will be able to use this data for marketing purposes either once, for a specific number of times, or until a specific date that is specified on the license agreement given to you by the data supplier at the time you buy the list. You'll need to keep this data on a separate list within your database so that you don't use it outside of the license agreement.

Bad data is anything collected in ANY other way that isn't one of the above. For example, you have just employed a new manager that used to work in another venue just up the road and she used to be in charge of their database. Before she left, she downloaded the database to take it with her. She may not know that what she has done is wrong. She worked hard to build the database, mostly on her own time, so she thinks that she has a right to take it with her.

You have employed a member of staff to search through Social Media platforms to find people of a certain who live in the local area. If they have either an email address or a mobile number on their profile, or both, the staff member is manually typing them into your database. Again the member of staff is happy to do this, oblivious that there's anything wrong with it, but these people have NOT given you permission to send them marketing communications.

In hospitality, the idea that not everyone is 'fair game' is a relatively new concept, especially for independents who have often have a 'scatter gun' approach to their marketing. First let me explain why you MUST adopt an innovative approach to Data Management, then I'll tell you why you should, and how it produces better results.

GDPR

Those four letters have been known to have a similar effect on people as an air-raid warning siren and sent them running for the hills. For marketing professionals, the *General Data Protection Regulations* are a thing to embrace and move forward from. For us they have the effect of levelling the playing field and making our arduous work and efforts actually count.

But wait, we've already followed the (relatively) new regulations by collecting our data in *only* the ways listed above right? These collection methods tie in with the legitimate reason for collecting and the use of data covered in GDPR, at least the ones that apply to us in hospitality, these are:

(1) Consent: the individual has given consent for you to process their personal data for a specific purpose – *e.g. entering a competition.*

(2) Contract: the processing is necessary for a contract you have with the individual – e.g. *a booking.*

(3) Legitimate interests: the processing is necessary for your legitimate interests – *e.g. they are a customer.*

49

The next two could apply to data that you have for your staff and the last one could apply as a result of a request from an official request.

(4) Legal obligation: the processing is necessary for you to follow the law (not including contractual obligations). *e.g. so that you can contact your staff*

(5) Vital interests: the processing is necessary to protect someone's life. *e.g. in relation to your health and safety policies*

(6) Public task: the processing is necessary for you to perform a task in the public interest or for your official functions, and the task or function has a clear basis in law. *e.g. an official request for data from the Police*

So now that you've had an introduction to this, if you want to look at it in more detail go to www.ico.org.uk which is an extremely useful source of information and you can register whilst you're there!

I mentioned earlier that there are other benefits to holding 'good' data, other than the obvious one – you're following the law and therefore there's no risk of a hefty fine. So we're not going to try to steal data that's not ours, solicit strangers that aren't interested in our venue, upload data from another venue or farm any other data from dodgy sources. If we don't do any of this, it stands to reason that what we're left with is good data. In other words it's for either our customers or people that have shown at least some interest in our venue or, in the case of bought data, they are exactly our target demographic and have 'opted in' via a third party data supplier. So when we carryout marketing activities with this data, it makes sense that we'll get a far better response rate than we would with bad data. Indeed, it's highly likely that we'd get exactly ZERO response from bad data, skewing our metrics and leaving us with no idea what was working or not.

Don't waste your time with bad data, you may get a pat on the back for having a large database, but in the long run you'll be wasting your time. It's a much better approach to put all of your efforts into collecting good data.

We will look at the practical ways to collect data as part of your marketing mechanics in Part Three.

Chapter Five
MARKETING TOOLKIT: PRINT

——————————— ◆◆◆ ———————————

P rinting is dead though isn't it, with everything done online these days…?

Whilst it's clearly true that venues don't rely on Print as much as they once did, Print is still alive and well, partly because there's still nothing stronger than a good flyer handed to a customer at the 'point of sale'.

I have had extensive first-hand experience of this over the past six years in my role as Marketing Director for Print company (with an actual print factory) that supplies Print to Hospitality businesses (and a few other sectors) right across the UK. It was my job to sell Print, but I have to tell you that every business that I dealt with on a daily basis knew the importance of print. I would advise on the offer, mechanic, design, size, quality and quantity; but our customers already knew that they needed Print. The problem in my job was to find the customers in the first place – everyone thinks they are getting the best In my experience at least, Print has become better value for money in the past ten years too... Increased choice and efficiency of digital print machines and more competition in the print industry has meant that print prices have not risen in line with inflation whilst the quality and speed of the goto print for our industry has improved dramatically.

Later we'll look at a checklist, which applies to multiple marketing channels, that covers what the *offer* should be on your print. For now, I would have you consider the need, the look and the feel of your printed material.

In August 1992, as the 'number two' at Chelteham Ritzy, and being of a certain age, I was tasked with attracting the freshers from the local college (as it was then – now much bigger and a University). It was a well-trodden path even back then but *my* first experience of the 'freshers fayre'. I can't recall the exact circumstances of why we were late organising the flyers; perhaps (on this occasion!) not my fault because I'd just moved up from Bristol. But late we were so it fell to me to turn these around in two days – no mean feat in 1992. It meant huge compromise for my first flyer design and print job and I wasn't happy about it. What we ended up with was a yellowish A6 (ish) flyer 1/0 – This is 'print-speak' for one colour, black and white; or in this case black and yellow!

I made the right connections at the college, arranged a 'free bus' to bring the freshers in from their campus and we stood at a trestle table with our crap flyers for a few hours.

What I'll never forget is a call with the area manager later in the day to brief him on how the preparations for our new night had been going. I felt like I had to come clean about the terrible flyers and take it on the chin. His response was a complete surprise to me. "Dean", he said in his signature tone which was both authoritarian and warm (how did he do that?), "If the offer is right, you could have printed it on toilet paper and it wouldn't matter".

Now I may have mentioned before that customers are more discerning these days, and that's actually progress isn't it? But he was right then and he is still right now. Sure, the design and quality of your print is an important factor. It makes a statement on who you are and, in a world, where customers act increasingly on an *emotional* level your print needs to make them *feel* good. The most important thing though is *the offer*...

The legal capacity of Cheltenham Ritzy was 850 people and to be honest, the fire exists were EXCEPTIONALLY good and so that was a bit of a squeeze. The college had 1500 freshers that year. They all turned up. At the same time. Before we opened.

Bath Road had to be closed because the pavement outside wasn't wide enough for the queue. We used the free bus that we'd hired to take customers from the back of this queue to our opposition club half a mile away in order to placate the local Police Inspector, who was not amused. His jolly Geordie accent had slipped into an official croak as his officers' time was taken up Policing our queue.

Let's not discuss the utter chaos that ensued inside the club because we simply let in too many people. That is a whole other story, for another time.

The point is that the (let's call it) resounding success of the launch was nothing to do with the actual flyer but the offer that it contained, the effort that went into getting it into the hands of the potential customers and the talks I had with the people that could influence them.

So, let's look at a checklist of things to mindfully ask yourself when you're putting together your print, before you push to the button to order it.

Does it have a real purpose for the business and what is that purpose?

It may sound a little obvious but I've lost count, over the years, of the number of times that I ordered print 'just because' that's the thing you do, without actually knowing what I was going to do with the flyers that were delivered. This is a yes or know and not hard to work out.

How will the print be distributed and for how long, therefore how many do I need?

If you intend to hand these out on your front door for five weeks and you have 2,000 customers every weekend, then you'll clearly need 10,000 printed and you'll get a decent price on 10,000 flyers. But if these are a takeaway menu or for a one-off night that's just two weeks away the likelihood is that you'll be left with a box after the event has passed and someone will need to dispose of them before they're seen by the person that pays the printer! If you're the person that pays the printer, you'll certainly have already thought of this.

Print Quote

Now that you know how many you need, you know which flavour of printer to use – a 'Lithographic' Printer (Litho) or a 'Digital' Printer. Knowing the difference between the two and knowing what any particular printer specialises in can save you some money because if you need Digital print and get this from Litho Printer, you may be paying over the odds, and vice-versa. In reality many Litho Printers may also have a Digital capability but specialist Digital printers will not have a Litho capability unles they farm it out, they will be smaller companies. Litho printers specialise in longer print runs and you'll get value out of runs of 5,000 and above. To enable them to do this they will have invested heavily in machinery and they must reach a certain print capacity. This means that if you're using one of these and you can give them a nice long lead time, you'll get even better value for money. It's a bit like booking a hotel… book long enough in advance and you'll probably get a good deal but the closer to the date that you need the more the price goes up. Then, there may be some nice last-minute discounts to fill the accommodation (print run) but in waiting for this you risk missing your deadline and getting your print too late.

Design

Considering the points above will give you some steer on design. Who will you use? Is it worth a top notch, expensive design job? Does it need to be in line with your venue's branding, or is it a new mini-brand of its own? Is there a particular designer who will 'get it' more than another? What sort of turnaround time do you need? What size will it be?

As a Hospitality owner you may already have become a bit of an expert on print because print is one of the biggest items on your P&L every year. You may have noticed that if you can cut the money spent on wasted print it goes straight to your bottom line! If you are experienced, you'll already be using a designer who speaks the same language as you, if you're not you need one. It's a particularly clever idea to stick to one designer that does speak your language and give them all of your work, that way, with a good designer, you'll earn their loyalty because this works both ways. Give a designer a wide berth if they tell you about all the amazing jobs they do every week for a massive client; chances are, when the chips are down, they'll jump through hoops for that client before opening your emails. Don't be afraid (or too proud) to get a second opinion on the design work that's been done for you. There's always someone with an opinion in our industry, on this occasion it may pay dividends to actually ask for it.

I could harp on about this for another chapter, but the point is that this all adds up to the need for planning when it comes to your design job. It may only take a designer two hours to produce an original design for your double sided A5 flyer, but when will that hour be? A good designer worth their salt isn't sitting at home playing video games waiting for your email and everyone else also has a deadline. So, planning means giving your design and print job more *time*. Build it in from the start and add a bit.

Proof Twice, Print Once

On day one of their apprenticeship, after being asked to buy a 'glass hammer', every trainee carpenter will have learned to 'measure twice and cut once'. The same is true when ordering print, just substitute 'measure' for 'proof' and 'cut' for 'print'. Definitely proof read anything that is being mass printed twice.

Proof read it yourself first and then ask someone else (who cares about it) to proof read it again. Pay particular attention to dates, phone numbers, email addresses, prices and offers. It is not the designers' job, or the printers' job to make sure that the details are accurate. It may be frustrating and you may be inclined to blame one of those for the mistake, but I'm afraid, the responsibility lies with you and you will be paying for the re-print.

Let me also give you a quick tip on what to do with your print when it arrives – open the box! This may seem obvious but, in my experience, perhaps 1% of the time (maybe less) there will be an issue with your delivery. If this is the case, the print company will fix the issue at their expense, but that won't help you if you've just found out on the day that you actually need the flyers.

A good practice is to take print out of boxes and onto a shelf with the rest of your print so that you can visually check what you have and when its running low.

I, of course, didn't do any of the above best practices when I was a young Manager in the nineties, which is why I can speak with such authority on the negative outcomes that you'll attract if you don't follow the simple advice. We had more time back then to learn the hard way and make some mistakes, not so today it seems, in a world that feels far more competitive – or maybe I just see it more clearly? Part of the reason for all of the moves to new venues when I was starting out was to allow for those mistakes, starting somewhere new every six months or so with a clean slate and considerably more knowledge. Because of these experiences I changed from the shy introvert trainee at just-turned-twenty-one, to the somewhat overconfident (with good reason as far as I was concerned) General Manager Designate at the still tender age of twenty-four. In three-and-a-bit short years I'd learned the basics of the trade under the wing of a good company with exceptionally good people and I'd only been sacked once, which probably bothered the person doing the sacking more than it did me, though not at the time. I also didn't realise at the time how much good it did me, "On this occasion".

Chapter Six
MARKETING TOOLKIT: EMAIL

L et's say that for your 1,000-capacity venue you have a database of 10,000 opted-in people. As we've seen before, this means that those people are either customers, have booked or are at the very least they are *interested* in your venue. Now consider that, if done correctly and using a tried and tested formula, so that you don't 'spam' your database, you could reach as many as 6,000 of those contacts each and every week for less than a daily *Skinny Vanilla Spice Latte.*

It's better than that, not only will you know exactly who opens your email and who clicks on your email but you'll also know *which link* they clicked.

Even better still, when you can automate emails based on what emails have been opened, where they have clicked or based upon a date of birth - the opportunities begin to multiply.

The opportunities for email marketing have also multiplied because of social trends. Smart phones aren't new these days but their popularity and usefulness continue to amaze as their everyday use trickles down (or up) through the age groups. This has meant that email has, albeit slowly, become a now useful tool for marketing to all target age groups in the hospitality sector from eighteen-year-olds to people in their seventies looking for the perfect Sunday Roast.

What you get for your marketing spend has also improved because of some other factors:

More people are accessing their emails on mobile devices compared to desktop computers.

This means that emails are checked more often and, as mentioned above, by all age groups, making it much easier to get your message through.

The way emails are displayed on smart phones is much improved.

You now get a highlighted 'from' line as well as subject line that can be personalised to increase open rates. You can also insert up to thirty words as a 'summary' of the email, especially useful to get your point across and a 'call to action'.

Email communications are part of the 'expected' norm.

In an earlier chapter I covered the need for good data and mentioned of the positive knock-on effect of this being good customer engagement. Here is where that good data, and all of the effort you put in to collect it, pays off. Your customers, and interested parties, will *expect* to get your emails and even *want* to get your emails. This means that your open rates will be good and the number of people that take action from your emails will be high. All of these people are effectively moving through your sales pipeline, not something that we ever talk about in a hospitality marketing setting, but happening all of the time nonetheless.

For these reasons, gone are the days of sending out 100,000 emails to bad lists to get terrible delivery rates and less than 5% open rates.

These days it's not unusual for my clients to get open rates of 35% or higher, with good click through rates and actual bookings straight away. You read that right Thirty-Five percent. I've had open rates as high as Sixty percent for new launches where great data has been collected and people are genuinely interested and *curious* about the venue.

Email marketing in hospitality has come of age. We'll look more closely at how to use it in Part Three.

Best practices for email communications:

Design. You could get your designer to create an HTML email for you. They will happily design a series of new images for one specific email communication, package them up and upload the code after a series of proofs in flat image format.

They will code the links and you'll have something beautiful as a result. There are several problems with this approach. First it will cost you. The likelihood is that your designer doesn't specialise in this so it will take them longer and a typical hourly rate for a designer of £45 can turn into a cost to you of £150 for one email design. If this is a central promotion covering multiple operating units, that's fine; but as a cost to a single unit for one email, it simply doesn't stack up. The other issue with this is one of lead time. I can create great looking email in around thirty minutes from scratch. If I'm using a template from a clone of an email that I've sent before I can do it in a fraction of that time – and you can too. Using a designer, the process will take a minimum of three days. Remember, good designers aren't waiting around all day for your call!

Personalisation. For people like me, who grew up before the internet was a thing, some of what can be achieved these days seems close to magic! What I'm interested in though are little add-ons that can have a great impact on both open rates and engagement without us getting into learning complicated new marketing techniques. Personalisation in emails is a great example of this. Using the Footfall Driver, it's very simple to insert your recipient's first name into the subject line of your email which has a direct impact on open rates and psychologically you're instantly attaching that person to your brand. In the body of the email, you can add further 'merge fields' for personalisation with a name or any other field that you have in your database. That's powerful, it doesn't cost anything extra, and it looks amazing.

Amount of information. No matter how popular your venue is and how interested your customers are, there's always a limit to how much information they will be willing to look at. Don't be tempted to try to tell them everything in one email, even if you feel like you have a lot to say. Limit your content to a maximum of three messages and don't write reams of text – unlike you, your customers haven't committed to reading a book! They will simply lose interest after the first long speech and the rest of the messages will be lost on them, whilst you believe that that information has gone out and been absorbed.

Above the fold. In website design when we talk about 'above the fold' we mean what the viewer can see on the webpage before they have to scroll down. This is the most valuable area and where your key message should appear (amongst other things). It's the same principle in email communications. Your main message and your key call to action should be visible before any scrolling is required because this may be the only information that your customer sees. This is especially important for the 'mobile' version of the email. These days, as with websites, what the recipient sees on a mobile will be optimised for mobile viewing and not exactly the same as on a desktop computer – because it's being viewed on a smaller screen it will be optimised for that.

Number of calls to action. Similar to the self-imposed limit that you'll set on the amount of information, you should really only have ONE clear call to action in your email, although this could be a "BOOK NOW" button that allows multiple options. Absolutely don't have more than TWO calls to action in one email.

Target it at the target audience. Seems obvious, but as already discussed, there's little point in sending your marketing emails to people who aren't remotely interested in them. How diverse your database is will depend on how diverse your sessions are. With many TCMY venues you'll send everything out to everyone, but if you have distinctive nights, for example aimed at the student population and others for people from that town or city, you would have segmented data and send to different lists accordingly.

Frequency of sends. Simple, don't send more than two emails a week or you customers will disengage, or worse still, opt out. You're not spamming, but it will feel like that to your customers and how they 'feel' is of utmost importance, don't do it!

Time of send. The platform that we use, The Footfall Driver, has a really clever integration that can optimise the send time individually for every customer. It actually sends the email at the time when it is most likely to be opened by your punters. That's a game changer and has resulted in far better open rates than we've ever seen before. If you don't have this feature on your platform, schedule them for 5:30pm – widely accepted as the best time to send an email. Or mix it up a little and monitor the results.

Chapter Seven
MARKETİNG TOOLKİT:
SHORT MESSAGE SERVİCE

SMS like email is now used increasingly right across the age spectrum. Five years ago, you wouldn't dream of targeting a text message campaign at the over 50's but now it's commonplace.

Operators that I've spoken to in Hospitality are roughly split down the middle when it comes to SMS marketing, half of them won't touch it and half probably use it far too much.

For the half that don't use it, and are likely to never be convinced, it's because of the cost. An SMS message, as part of an integrated platform costs around 4p to send. Not much, you may think, but if you have a database of 20,000 then a send to all of them will set you back a cool £800. In our business, that better be a message that generates revenue pretty quickly, right?

There is a case and a place for text messaging though, because of one indisputable fact:

When people receive a text message, *they will definitely see it* if it is delivered, and Ninety-Nine percent of text messages will be delivered. So, when the most important task is to get the message through the fog of the day-to-day communications that everyone receives, then SMS is the way.

I have been using SMS marketing for twelve years. The number of characters that you get to work with hasn't changed during that time – 160. That sounds a lot but it's a surprisingly sparce amount when you start trying to cram in everything you want to say on your 4p message and it's an artform to get it exactly right.

In SMS you need to keep things simple, you'll need one call to action, two at most. Not only because of the limiting number of characters that you have to work with, which will most likely be even less than 160 because of the legal requirement for an 'opt-out' at the foot of the message. But also because there's a limit to the attention span of your recipients when reading a text message. Please also note that most platforms will allow you to go over 160 characters, but you'll spill over into a second message which will cost you another 4p. You really don't want this to happen just because you weren't paying enough attention yourself!

'Text speak'

It's easy to get caught up in your skills with creating 160-character text messages for your customers, and in doing so making them completely unreadable for your target market...

If your marketing is targeted at an eighteen to twenty-two audience something like this would be fine:

"2-4-1 shots 2night @ Venue + arrive b4 9pm 4 ur chance 2 win a £50 bar tab for u and ur m8s!"

This would of course be completely inappropriate for, say, an over fifties audience who may even be offended by it – not what we're trying to achieve at all!

The general rule is that when writing your messages, you need to mirror the type of language that the target age group would use. This takes precedence even over the content of the offer because if they don't read the message the content is irrelevant.

The best formula that I use for SMS marketing is one call to action and one weblink. You'll find that many platforms use a link shortening tool to turn a long URL into an abbreviated bespoke link. Some people are wary of these links because they look dodgy and they believe that people are less likely to click on them. My own opinion is that whereas people used to be cautious of links like this they are less so these days, especially if you're using good, opted-in data and you've used your venue's name in the 'from' section.

Whatever you're sending to your customers, it will always feel like you don't have enough characters to play with and you need more. You'll always need to compromise and prioritise your main driver for the message. This can have the effect of actually focussing your mind on what the real objective is for the message and whether or not SMS is the right channel. In any event, you won't pay for the messages until you clicked 'send', so you'll be able to deliberate over what to send until you're completely happy.

There's some debate on what type of number to use as a 'from' number for your SMS marketing. Platforms will allow you to choose a number which can either be a mobile number or a landline. Again, people are split fairly evenly on which is best or worst, but I don't think that right now there's any good evidence either way, so just go with what you feel best suits your business.

When you send an SMS, message is an important thing to consider and this will depend largely on what the objective is for the message. If you have a particular space to fill in your restaurant from a cancelled booking then that will dictate when the message goes out. Equally if you're having a 'flash sale' that will also be an indicator. If however you're launching a new session, you'll need to think carefully about timing and how the SMS fits in with your wider marketing campaign.

There are platforms that offer a 'landing page' function and I have had first-hand experience of using these because in a previous version of the *Footfall Driver*, which is the platform that my customers use, we had that functionality. However, in that case, the software had gone one step too far in my opinion (which is partly why we use a different system now). The fact was that nobody used this functionality because it was a bit 'fiddly', took time to learn and had one or two glitches. Mostly though they didn't use it because what's the point in creating a new landing page to link to from the message when EVERY business already has a website that they can point to? Answer: none. Furthermore, one of the objectives of a new landing page would be to get people to click through to where you ultimately wanted them to go, so why not point them straight there from the text message? This is just another example of learning as we go!

Chapter Eight
MARKETING TOOLKIT: KEYWORD CAMPAIGNS

————— ◆◆◆ —————

S MS keyword campaigns are an extremely useful tool that can be used in a multitude of ways, some of which we'll look at in detail in Part Three as we delve into some marketing mechanics.

For those of you with no experience of Keyword Campaigns, they are messages triggered to send to a person after *they* have sent a 'keyword' message by text to a particular number from their device. Essentially, they are a tool to be used for people to respond quickly and easily to a 'call to action'.

To set these up is relatively inexpensive and, once set up, they will only cost you marketing budget if they are used by your customers. Hence, they have been used very successfully for, amongst others, 'guest lists' as well as for new venue launches and competition entries. A side benefit of a keyword campaign is that you get to keep the data and you also know exactly where it came from making segmentation much easier.

It's a good idea to have a fixed start and finish time and date for your keyword campaigns. For the start this is so that you and your team know when to expect responses and are geared up to take the necessary action to deal with those responses. A definite finish time and date is necessary so that you're not getting responses after your activity has ended. The platform I use will allow you to automate the start and finish times so that you don't need to remember to cancel them. Keyword campaigns really come into their own in a hospitality setting when they form part of a strategy with a mechanic – we'll look at a couple of examples of these in Part Three…

Chapter Nine
Marketing Toolkit:
A Summary

Now, you will have noticed that, as I mentioned in Chapter 3 (Why you need to collect data) I haven't discussed 'Social Media' as part of your Marketing Toolkit. As I also previously said, this is deliberate because it's highly likely that you already know everything that you need to know to implement the Marketing Mechanics that contain an element of social media. I am not an advocate of paid social media marketing, for the reasons that I set out before, but it does have a place and we'll look at that place soon.

So, here's a list of marketing tools that we do use followed by a list of more marketing tools that we won't use in Marketing Mechanics covered in Part Three…

Database – Yes, everything starts with good data.

Print – Yes, in many different forms that we will look at, including direct mail and leaflet distribution.

Email – Yes, email has come of age, it's versatile and you can measure results easily.

SMS – Yes, it has its place but needs to be targeted *or* part of exactly the right mechanic to be cost-effective.

Keyword Campaigns – Yes

Social Media – Yes. Similar to the need for a website, you'll need a social media presence on the platforms that fit your audience and you will use them for some mechanics, but not paid advertising.

Publications – No. Look, if you have a local publication that you love, or more to the point *is loved by your target audience,* it's a perfect fit for your business and, with an honest, emotion-free look at it, you can quantify and justify the expense with a guaranteed return on investment, then crack on.

Mac Kulesza – Powerhouse Birmingham - 1983

Ritzy Torquay – 1990

Event II – West Street, Brighton - 2001

Liquid Gloucester – 2002

The dancefloor from the DJ console, Liquid

PART THREE

Mechanics

Chapter Ten
DRIVE DATA COLLECTION

⸺⸺⸺ ⸭ ⟩◆⟨ ⸭ ⸺⸺⸺

When we talk about 'Mechanics' we mean the mechanism behind how the pieces of the marketing activities fit together to create a coherent set of promotional activities that work to drive footfall into your venue. Everything we do is geared up for this and more people and more profits are the *whole* point. If you don't have that, nothing else really matters because you don't have a viable business!

Many of the marketing mechanics that we'll look at will have the added benefit of collecting data, but what do you need to do if you're starting with zero data? Collect some as soon as possible! Using my platform, 'The Footfall Driver' as an example of a database tool here are ten ways to get you started at collecting data. In every example you'll need a strong reason for people to enter their data. What that reason is, or more to the point how strong the 'call to action' needs to be, is up to you to decide. This is marketing in its purest form. On one extreme are customers throwing themselves at you because they are desperate to know what's happening in your shiny new venue that everyone is already talking about, so they'll part with their details with the merest hint of being able to get information about you when you deem to release it. On the other extreme, are people either completely oblivious to your existence or deeply sceptical about what you have to offer and so need a strong incentive, usually a 'free thing' or a competition entry, to even contemplate filling in a form?

Give this some thought and discuss with anybody who may have an opinion. Remember though that you can always increase the incentive, if necessary, but it's harder to take it away if you've already given it.

1. **The contact form on your website.** If you built your own website, you'll already have the skills to integrate the iframe HTML code into your site. If this is all a foreign language to you, don't worry, for your web developer this is a simple task without the need for any coding – that's already all done for you, even the formatting of the form is done. From this form you'll get a notification email when someone fills it in and you get to store the data in the contact list of your choice. You can set up as many of these as you want, so even though your website could look like it's got the same form on every page that it appears, it could be a different form on every page, allowing you to segment

your data depending on what page visitors have landed on. In turn this will let you target your email and SMS marketing more effectively.

2. **Export the data from your online booking system.** Upload it to your database, then look to link your booking system to your database via an API (application programming interface). This is a fancy name for the link between your two software platforms, your database platform your bookings platform.

3. **Use a customer WiFi system that collects data.** For a set-up fee and then around £30 per month you can have a customer Wifi system that requires a login from its users. This good practice even if you're not collecting data because it allows you to control who can log in and how much data they can download and upload. With a good system, you'll also be able to see new logins versus returning customers, gender ratio and dwell times. You'll be able to create a bespoke landing page and also send automatic message, if want to, to customers who log in. Most importantly customers will be able to 'opt-in' to receive marketing and, from real statistics from my customers, around seventy percent of your customer will do so. Furthermore, over multiple visits, around seventy percent of your customers will log into your customer WiFi, a figure that you can increase

with good signage in your venue. If you have, say one-thousand customers, how many other methods to you have of getting data for half of them on autopilot, without lifting a finger? To coin two phrases that I hate, this is a win, win no brainer.

4. **Set up a 'Keyword Campaign'.** This could be as simple as texting a keyword to your number for more information on your venue, if you're in the scenario where everyone wants a piece of you. In this way you're getting their data and permission to send them information. The method of data capture, as in all cases, will be recorded so that you have a strong (a legal) audit trail for where the data was acquired and, as ever, you can put the data into your desired list for segmentation.

5. **QR code linked to a form.** Similar to a barcode used to label products, QR codes are a two dimensional 'optical label' which link the scanner to a web URL – our forms will be hosted on a URL. When you use a QR code you're just asking you're customers to fill in a form again, however it's all about the flexibility of where and how you can do this, so for a number of reasons QR codes are an excellent choice of tool: 'QR' stands for 'Quick Response' Whilst only a few short years ago QR codes were seen by many as too 'techy' for marketing they too have now really come of age.

This is partly due to improvements in mobile phone technology, now you only need open your camera and point it at the QR code, as if taking a picture and the link will pop up, one click and you're into the form. It is precisely because of their ease of use that they have started to become mainstream, being used, as with mobile devices themselves, by all and sundry. Oddly they have also been brought to the fore by the *Global Pandemic,* being used by the UK Government's track and trace system which has effectively mopped up the few sceptical stragglers that remained oblivious to QR codes and created the need to embrace them as an 'everyday' tool. Here's an example of a QR code that links to a form, it will also add you to my mailing list!

6. **Tablet form for your staff to collect data from customers.** There's still nothing quite like a human

being interacting with you and asking you to answer a question, especially if done the right way, in a pleasant manner with a little incentive at the end. Good, old fashioned, sales. So near to the start of your session, when things are still warming up, your staff aren't all that busy yet and customers are trickling in, why not send one of your staff with some communication skills out there with a tablet connected to your WiFi to ask your customers for their details – perhaps just to keep them in the loop with your newest offers. Or maybe to enter a competition to win a 'free thing' that they can only enter because they arrived early? These people, after all, are probably your best customers and you want them to stick around. The benefits in doing this far outweigh just getting the data. Any interaction with your best customers is priceless AND can create a buzz. Trust me your competitors will not be doing this, it's extremely easy to do but very few operators will ever do it!

7. **Upload spreadsheets from an existing database**. If you do have any good data knocking around make sure that you upload it before you collect any more data and label it accordingly. My advice would be to keep it separate from the new stuff and do a couple of test campaigns targeting just this to see how good it

actually is.

As I mentioned at the start of this chapter, everything else that we do will also drive data, but get all of the above in place first and you'll be covering all of your bases. This is all about maximising your ability to reach people consistently and exactly when you need and want to that the effectiveness of your marketing communications stands head and shoulders above your competition. The best bit is that most of the above, once implemented, will be on autopilot, generating you new, fresh data whilst you sleep.

Chapter Eleven
NEW OPENINGS & RELAUNCHES

━━━━━━━━━━ ◆◈◆ ◆ ━━━━━━━━

These two are grouped in together because when your open a new venue you'll want to create a buzz and let people know what they can expect from your new venue. You'll highlight that you're the best new thing in town, you will be popular (people go where people are) and you'll be doing it bigger and better than it's been done before! This is exactly the same for a relaunch, or there would be no point in relaunching. Something, *most things* need to have changed and you'll approach the marketing in the same way as if you were opening a new venue.

Let me share with you now what one of my biggest customers does when they open a venue. This isn't a one-off opening but a tried and tested method that they employ and have used for every one of 36 openings of new late-night venues that they have launched in the past ten years. They have also used these methods for relaunches that they have done numerous times also over the past seven years. So during the past ten years the number of combined openings and relaunches that they've done is probably around eighty.

What always impressed me about this operator and the people that they had at the top was that they each had defined specialist roles in their area of expertise: Property, People Management, Marketing Strategy, Marketing Implementation, Purchasing and Area Operations Management, to name a few. Furthermore, all of these roles slotted together into a coherent, well-oiled machine that just worked. By the time they had agreed terms on a location for their next venue they already knew that the demographics of the area were spot on, they knew which of their strong brands it would suit best, they knew who the manager would be, what the price points would be, what level of offer was needed to launch with and son. All of these decisions had been made, all that was left was to push the button. For these reasons only two out of 36 venue launches failed in the long term, in the short term they were all a success. In other words, they opened to a capacity crowd.

Incidentally, at the time of writing we have a date on which late-night venues can (or are likely to be able to) open after lockdown three in the UK. Whilst many of the corporates and independents are still busy whinging about the effects of the lockdown, these people are getting on with it. They have decided to launch their newest venue on the first day that they can legally open (a Monday by the way) and they are going full tilt at promoting it even though the date is still over three and a half months away. That's how you launch a venue.

So, what do they always do?

Well, besides getting every other area right, which I know isn't easy but we're focussing on marketing here, they always had the following elements to their venue launch campaigns.

1. **They signed up to a new digital marketing platform.** In this case my platform, The Footfall Driver.

2. **They booked a Customer WiFi installation.** This was then linked straight away to their Footfall Driver for data capture.

3. **They began to collect data as soon as the opening was announced.** In fact, collecting data is *the reason* for the announcement of the date that the venue will open. This was done via a Keyword campaign to get onto the guestlist for one of the opening weekend nights by texting "Friday" or "Saturday" plus your name to the short code or mobile number. Notice that they haven't also asked for an email address yet. Generally, people get spooked (or bored) if you ask them for too much data at one time. That's why you'll notice that when you're signing up for just about any kind of membership, or even buying something online, you're usually sent to multiple screens before you've given

enough information to finally get what you want. If you saw a huge screen in front of you with blanks to fill in you may give up before you've started. They will also have launched their new website at the same time and added multiple data entry points therein for different offers, another way to get onto the opening weekends guestlists and the classic "something to celebrate?" – in reality just another a contact form.

4. **Social Media.** They will also of course have their social media pages up together, in the case of this type of late-night venue they have Facebook, Twitter and Instagram accounts. On all of these they will be running competitions to win a 'VIP' experience on the opening weekend *without* paid advertising. This will collect data and they will also have the usual form links to sign up for "the latest information". They'll also be doing a daily countdown with all of the hype they can muster!

5. **Mailshot.** Whilst creating hype on Social Media is a promising idea, when all's said and done everyone else, as I motioned at length before, is also doing that. More is needed and for this operator a key investment into their launches has always been a mail drop. The exact formula that they put into the investment of the mail drop will depend upon the budget available for

the whole project. I'm sure you realise, if you choose to give it some logical thought, that you shouldn't spend £100,000 refurbishing your venue and then spend £50 marketing it – if you build it, they will not come! In reality the amount spent should come from the available demographic. What this operator does is to buy in ALL of the available data for females within a ten-mile radius, between the ages of nineteen and (usually, depending on the area) twenty-eight. In years gone by we used to be able to get data for new eighteen-year-olds but this isn't possible anymore because of modern data restrictions and it's not a particularly clever idea anyway these days because eighteen-year-olds have seventeen-year-old friends. Licensing laws are far stricter these days, everyone gets their ID checked on the way in and leaving seventeen-year-olds out on the street is an unbelievably bad idea (almost as bad as letting them in).

The content of the mailer is also a set formula that has evolved over a ten-year period.

First of all, its posted in a white, A5 window envelope. White because we don't want it to look like a bill or a letter from HMRC! A5 because you can then insert a three-part colour folded mailing piece with a combined surface area the equivalent to three sides of A4 paper – easily enough room for your extended message in a good-sized font that can be easily read. And finally a window envelope so that we can mail-merge the data that we have when it is digitally printed which is cost and visually effective. The mailer will be digitally merged with the recipient's name in several places for a sublime distinctive touch that is proven to engage more people, it makes them feel special. Anything that invokes feelings in marketing is particularly good for our cause.

I've already discussed design and the need for it to be very good - and good not just in your opinion. Remember, it costs exactly the same to print a bad design as it does to print a good one, so get this right. This is never more important than when the message is being sent to a potential customer at home and is their first impression of you.

Of course, before you can embark on design, you'll need to know what the offers are. In the case of our protagonists there are always three levels of offers and again, this is a tried and tested method that works.

With some regional variations in actual pricing levels, the three offers contained in the mailing piece that will be sent to at least five-thousand recipients are...

Level One: The instant offer with very little action necessary – just turn up. This is achieved by including a set of tickets – usually six, as a good number for a small party, either as part of the mailing piece itself or as an extra printed insert of perforated tickets. The point is that no further planning, money changing hands or interaction is required, it couldn't be simpler. Usually free admission before a cut off time when you hand in the ticket you have brought with you.

Level Two: The planned visit. The customer needs to text you to get an offer that's a bit better than just free admission before a certain time – perhaps a reserved area or a bottle of bubbly for your party of six or more. The premise here is that the customer does need to take some action and that action is achieved via a keyword campaign (or more than one for multiple nights). So text your name plus the keyword to the advertised number. The customer gets a text back with details of the offer and you get a notification of the interaction AND you get to store and keep the customer's data for future marketing. You can also add the name to the official guest list that's printed out and given to staff on your front door.

Level Three: The 'Buy-in' offer. The is the Holy Grail for operators as it's effectively a commitment from the customers to visit your venue because they have advanced-purchased something. This could also be a reserved booth VIP area, depending on your popularity. Or it could be an offer on a pre-purchased drinks or food package. even, of course a pre-paid entry ticket. In the early part of my career the only advance ticket sales would be for New Years Eve and on that night every year the spend per head would double. That's simply because if customers have already paid for their entry ticket in advance they are likely to spend more with you than they normally would, a very straightforward idea but one that shows the potential of advance sales that has now been tapped into by savvy operators worldwide.

Think of these three offers as a kind of sales funnel. At the top you have the easy-entry offer that's likely to be the option for the masses. Lower down then, with a naturally smaller uptake is the first offer where customers need to take some action, but the action is simple and, of course, free. Then finally you have the offer where you customers are committing by parting with their cash. These will be far fewer but great to have and the foundation of both your revenue and footfall for your launch nights. All of these offers are designed to launch your brand as well as capture sales.

As you can see, the mailshot is a significant investment, but they are only doing this once for a launch or a re-launch and they get it right with no half measures. They have one chance at the opening, there are no dress rehearsals and no awards for second place, only a failed business. What they do before the opening day will have repercussions for the next three years of trading, so it's VITAL to get it right.

To put this into context though, this is THE main

marketing expense of the launch but it's affordable as much because of what they aren't doing as the good returns that they get from it.

6. **Networking.** This is really all about making friends and influencing people. My clients employ what they call a 'hit team' of like-minded individuals whose job it is to go to the launch towns and blitz it with networking. They will contact ALL of the businesses in that town where their target age groups work, for example hairdressers, gyms, coffee shops, clothes retailers and beauty salons. All of these people will be invited to the launch night VIP experience and all of them will be talking about it. It's like the ultimate contrived let. Nothing is left to chance. You'll need your own 'hit team' but look, why not just take on some of your staff a bit early? By the time you actually open they will be invested in your business and they will already have learned to function as a team. From the point of view of staff, openings are always great fun and by doing this you can take away some of the pressure that you'll feel from the point of view of an owner or manager.

When they launch their next venue they won't be doing any of the following....

Bus side advertising

Poster site advertising

Newspaper advertising

Magazine advertising

Radio Advertising

All of these could have some merit, but the point is they aren't measurable, and they are 'above the line' and, if you remember, *we don't do above the line.*

If you have any kind of experience marketing in hospitality, with hand on heart you know that newspaper and magazine advertising is a waste of money, don't you?

These, and only these, are the key elements to every launch that this customer of mine has ever done. You're forgiven for thinking that these are very simple and straightforward, they are, but that's what marketing in the hospitality sector is all about... doing the simple things consistently and doing them well. Generally, I hate anachronyms, but here's one that I learnt in my first six months as a management trainee:

K.I.S.S. Keep It Simple Stupid

The above formulaic approach can be adjusted and used for opening any other genre of hospitality venue. Just change the target data, offers and artwork for your mailer and use the right social media platform for your age group.

Another tool that's completely free, invaluable and I've

always used is the 'Critical Path'. It's a timeline, built by you that (usually) ends at your launch night, although you may want to extend it into the first six weeks of your operation. It contains everything in order leading up to a launch that you deem 'CRITICAL' to success. In fairness this isn't unique to the hospitality sector or even business.

So, this is essentially a calendar with all of the tasks that you need to do prior to your launch. We're looking at the marketing critical path ending in a launch date and we'll always start at the launch date and work backwards. I'd suggest producing this critical path as soon as you've decided on a relaunch date or an opening date. Working backwards from the launch towards the present date will quickly tell you whether your launch date is realistic.

As just one example of what would be in this critical path... your mailout will need to hit the doormats of your prospective customers at least four clear weeks before the target opening date. This is so that they have time to engage with your call to action after digesting the promotional material and organise things with friends for a social event. For big PA's this should be extended to six weeks and for larger events like festivals, at least six months.

So, for our example we intend to launch on 21st June (very topical in the UK). our mailer, in this example, will need to hit doormats on 24th May and typically the mail will take 5 working days to arrive using mailsort which (for the sake of a bit more organisation) will save us £2,800 on a typical 5,000 mailshot! You have read that right... Currently in the UK a first-class stamp costs 85p but mailsort postage for the quantities we're looking at (and less) is currently just 29p. For less than the cost of a first-class stamp you can buy the data and have the mailer printed and all of the work done for you. Allowing for weekends (non working days for everyone else!) the mailer posting date is then set at 17th May. Check with your mailing house on their lead times. I've known some to be extremely quick, recently I sent a 700 mailer out in four days which included some changes to artwork. For our example let's say they've guaranteed a four day turnaround, now build in an extra two days for amendments (like mine). This means that they will need to have completed artwork and data by 6th May. The two elements that they need can be done using the same timeline of course, let's look at the artwork bit., that will take the most time, but also ad 'data' to your critical path, because you don't want to get your artwork back on time only to be held up for two days buying in the data.

And so to artwork again. This is more complicated than your average piece of artwork for sure but let's first work backwards from when your designer sends you the completed

print ready piece. How long would you allow fo
giving them a concise brief. For the sake of this e>
say that your designer knows exactly what she or he is doing
and will take five working days to complete it, allowing for
amendments. You need to give your designer a concise brief
by 28th April. Generally this mailer will be an amalgamation of
all of your other artwork and offers put together. So in order
for you to give this brief you'll need to know exactly what your
offering is for every session and already have pricing structures
in place. This in turn may be the subject of some debate for
while as you apply these prices to your budgets to form some
realistic targets. let's leave the critcal path there shall we? I'm
sure you get the message – get organised.

We're looking at generating Footfall with all of these
techniques, keeping things very simple and really only paying
lip service to the other big element of marketing – finding your
target market and getting your offer right. By 'offer' I mean
the whole concept: price structures, the tangible things you
sell (food, beer, wine, champagne) and the *experiences* you sell
through the atmosphere and aesthetics of your venue and the
people that you employ to deliver the service standard you
aspire to.

In no small way though, in adopting tried and tested
methods to drive footfall, you'll be forced to take a long hard

look at your concept all of the time. You'll tweak it along the way as you aim for the Moon and sometimes this with throw up some surprises.

Let's look at some other examples of how what I've outlined in this Chapter can be adjusted to suit other marketing needs...

Chapter Twelve
SPECIAL EVENTS

——— ◆◆◆ ———

We'll assume for this that you've already launched or re-launched your venue – otherwise refer back to the above process.

So, you've decided to put a big act on in your venue. The definition of a 'big act' for you will really depend on where in the world you are, how big your venue is and what your spend per head is.

There are several reasons to put on something big too. You could be launching a new session. You may just be going for more Footfall on an existing session. It could be to highlight your venue with more awareness or it *could* be a way to generate more profit *if* you've done your research and you have a detailed budget. I wouldn't rely too heavily on the last one though, whilst the effect of a big act is usually very positive, the price of acts are driven by market forces and you're unlikely to hit a gold mine.

I would be cautious too about putting on acts too often if they don't stack up financially...

I once did a nightclub launch where we had planned six big acts in the first six nights (Fridays and Saturdays over two weeks). I'm not sure if I should mention names? Oh, go on then, I'm certainly not saying anything detrimental about the artists, they were all fantastic and great crowd-pullers. I won't tell you how much they cost though, but you'll get an idea.

On the first night *Danny Dyer* came along for a personal appearance. We were at capacity by around 9:30pm, there was a huge buzz in the town and local TV picked it up as well as local newspapers. From my point of view as one of the venue managers at the time it was great to be a part of this, especially in a small seaside town where this sort of thing doesn't happen every day. There were, however, in hindsight, a couple of issues! The fee was approximately the same as the night's gross takings, so take out the cost of sales alone and we made a loss. Not in itself a massive issue, it was a loss-leader, right? It achieved its objective of filling the venue on its first night. Well yes, but it filled the venue with (basically) thirty-something Ladies who were in love with Danny Dyer and thirty-something blokes who wanted to have a pint with him. It doesn't take a genius to realise that these weren't our target audience, even if some of them really loved the idea of clubbing into their forties, only a very few would visit us more than twice a year.

On the second night Ollie Murs, straight out of his X Factor live shows, came along for a meet and greet and sang a few songs on stage to captivated full-house number two. We hit a bit of luck with Ollie as we had booked him well in advance but then he did very well on the show and was probably the public's favourite even though he came second. Because we booked him a long way ahead he was cheaper but still contractually obliged to turn up. If we had booked him the following week to come back, he would have cost as much as Danny Dyer.

Unfortunately, I didn't have a pint with Danny Dyer but he was a very nice bloke. Ollie was also a good bloke who told me that I looked like Mark Chapman (the TV presenter, not the guy who shot John Lennon). I said I was happy with that because 'Chappers' is ten years younger than me. Actually he's only five years younger than me.

The following Friday we had booked prominent Radio One Dance DJ. I loved this, but our potential customer, not so much. It was our first bad night because in small towns, nightclubs with a capacity of over one-thousand need to be more mainstream by definition. These DJs are far too 'serious' for a mainstream crowd to stay for more than an hour. It's simply not enough *fun*. We had our first bad night.

The second Saturday night saw Danyl Johnson with us for

a stage performance. Danyl was also hot on the heels of the X Factor live shows, where he reached the semi-final. You know Danyl, the one who now does the 'Poscode Lottery' adverts on TV – lovely bloke.

Here's where things started to go a little awry...

Whilst these were all great acts, as I mentioned earlier, we weren't really pulling in our target audience and by week two the thirty-somethings were flagging meaning that we didn't quite hit capacity on the second Saturday night. For the following weekend we had 'Basshunter' booked for Friday night and Alexandra Burke booked for Saturday night. But the owner was beginning to get cold feet about Alexandra and we all had a meeting where it was decided that throwing another night's gross takings at it was a bad idea.

Basshunter went ahead, Alexandra Burke didn't. Shame.

Basshunter was a really great fit for us being more of a mainstream dance act and Jonas was well known for giving a great stage performance in clubs. He arrived early because he was doing a double gig for us. One for the under eighteens session from 7pm and then one for our main session starting at 10:30pm to our adult crowd.

I had been warned by the club's owner, who knew Jonas, not to let him leave the club between the performances. Apparently, he "liked a drink" and had been known to scupper his own chances of actually making it to a late performance if he got a taste for it. I had an initial conversation bringing this up with Jonas' manager before the first gig. He assured me that he would look after our investment and that it would be fine.

To my horror, a wired Jonas left through our back door straight after the first show with his manager in tow. I exchanged a few titled eyebrow knowing glances with said manager as they disappeared down the dark alleyway at the back of the venue.

Three hours later I was nervous. We had opened and were expecting a capcity crowd. Basshunter were on stage in less than an hour's time and Jonas and his manager were nowhere to be seen. I get a call on the radio to say that Jonas had been spotted near the entrance to the rear alleyway and it didn't look good.

I ran out of the back door to see Jonas, staggering toward me, held up by his manager, head down and bobbing from side to side as they approached...

Then he lifted his head, beamed at me, slapped me on the back and in his American Swedish accent said: "got you man". They both fell about laughing and I was too relieved to be annoyed. The act was awesome, we should have booked him for the opening night (no offence Danny).

We had to cancel Alexandra, it just didn't stack up, but then this had other effects that we weren't anticipating. Cancelling an act that we had already started to promote had a negative impact on the whole plan. It also highlighted the fact that people were now expecting us to have live acts every week and were actually disappointed and critical if we didn't have one! This wasn't the outcome that we wanted at all. Fortunately, I realised exactly what went wrong and you can learn from it at much less expense.

So, the moral of this particular story is that you need to know precisely *why* you're putting an act on before you even start thinking about the what, how and when. It goes without saying that the why shouldn't have any emotion attached to it on your part. It's your customers that need to have the emotional response, most definitely NOT you, tempting as it may be to put on an act that you'll love and that will add a couple of nice stories to your book fifteen years later.

Let's get back to the how to market your event from the point at which you've selected a great act that will pull the right customers at the right price, using the formula that we've already looked at to launch a venue with a few tweaks, from the top...

1. Digital Marketing – You already have a decent database by now because your digital platform has been up and running collecting data since your launch. If you've been around for a few years and business is harder (because you're no longer the shiny new venue) or

you're fighting off new competition, this is where your efforts in regularly and systematically collecting your customer's data over the past three years is about to pay off for you, simply because now you really need it to get that message out. Send an email out straight away, as soon as the act is booked, with an early-bird offer for advance tickets.

2. You already have customer WiFi. Use it to send a BounceBack message to everyone who visits in the next few weeks before your event. Add a link to the ticket buying page of your website. Your customers can get this the next morning after their visit.

3. Collect more data via forms on QR codes printed on your advertising flyers. This could be in the form of a competition to win tickets and then you can use the data to email them in the lead up.

4. Social media – obviously! (You know what to do – don't pay for it!)

5. Mailshot – The method described above was for launches. But if you already have birthday mailers going out on a regular basis, throw in a flyer. And if you're planning a series of events, for example for the Summer Bank holidays, then a specific mailer for several bits of activity might be a good use of your marketing budget.

6. Networking – You already have a great network because you set this up when you launched, since then you've nurtured them and they are happy to help you to spread the word, make sure they are the first to know and this relationship will get even better.

7. Critical Path? - Absolutely. If you've done one for a launch then this will be much easier, but still a very useful management tool.

8. Get busy – hopefully by now you can see why I keep mentioning that. I also hope that by now all of this stuff is less daunting because you have more direction?

Well done your event was a huge success, you get a small bonus, the owners like you and you don't have to move your family to a different town.

Chapter Thirteen
BRINGING IT ALL TOGETHER

———— ◆◆◆ ————

I t's up to you which of these tried and tested strategies, used by countless highly successful venue operators in the country, that you decide to use. Once again, in case you missed it the tenth time, the most important message here is to take action and, to some extent, take measured risks. Have you ever wondered why many of the best venue managers in entrepreneurial settings are below thirty-five? This may be a bit of an over-simplification, but, in my long experience, over time managers get jaded by marketing. They have tried everything and, as is the nature in marketing, at one point or another, most things would either have failed to work or its been impossible to quantify their level of success.

Human nature then takes over and managers become extremely wary of attempting to do these marketing activities again because there is enough empirical evidence that it wouldn't be a complete waste of time and money. In marketing, 'playing it safe' usually means doing nothing, or doing something like putting a quarter page advert in the local newspaper for less than a hundred quid. Managers can convince themselves that by doing no marketing the business has become magically more profitable.

This scenario is likely to crop up regardless of whether you're a manager in a corporate chain setting or the owner-manager of a hospitality business.

If you're the former you've probably been placed under serious pressure at some point in your career, held accountable for expensive marketing activity that's not delivered, or, even worse, used your entire budget up too fast and been told to freeze marketing activity until year end.

If you're an owner-manager it can often feel like the marketing budget comes out of your own pocket so if something doesn't work once, there's no incentive to repeat the process.

The best way by far to combat this 'marketing fatigue' is by taking action to formulate a coherent plan. The very best Entreprenurial managers that I've ever known have come through these difficulties and are still incredibly proactive marketers. They have achieved this by naturally having or cultivating the following attributes:

1. They have a plan and take action.

2. They are open to new ideas and ways of doing things.

3. They don't try to do everything themselves.

4. They build teams of talented people who they reward accordingly.

5. They brush off failures and regard them as part of the learning process.

6. They constantly evaluate the effectiveness of campaigns.

7. They are constantly learning.

Before I became a general manager myself (almost twenty-eight years ago now!) I was 'exposed' to a number of great General Managers and Area Managers whose expertise rubbed off on me and I was very fortunate that the first one was particularly good.

Most of them seemed to be very good at their special blend of entrepreneurial marketing in those days, it was a prerequisite for the job back then. They were truly 'old school' and had probably fought their way to the positions that they had through hard work, grit and determination. Rank Leisure was born out of Mecca Leisure in the late Eighties and many of its managers were from the old Dancehall Suites in the North of England.

By the North of England, having been born in South Devon, growing up there and living there until I was 21, that means anywhere north of Bristol. We're a bit funny down here!

117

I went to a Torquay United home game a few years ago where the home fans were chanting "You dirty northern ba***rds at the away fans", from Southend!

I suspect that the management style that embraced the 'showman' in these individuals who sold escapism and fun every weekend rubbed off on the South, where I was, and captivated a generation who found themselves with more money in their pockets than our friends in the North. Easy pickings for Managers well used to trying to fill venues in South Yorkshire, Humberside and the Wirral.

On page XXX there's a photo of one such 'Northern Manager', though actually only as far north as Birmingham (so in fact a Midlands boy). In 1983 Mac Kuleza was the General Manager of The Powerhouse in Birmingham, a famous old venue and one of the first of its kind. Ten years later he would be one of my first General Managers at 5th Avenue in Southsea. A great guy with a wealth of industry knowledge. His lovely wife Tess used to cook the management team a wonderful Sunday lunch!

One night, during the two formative years that I spent in Pompey, Mac had booked Edwin Starr for a live performance on the make-shift box stage in front of the DJ console. In fact this was the second time in eighteen months that Edwin had performed for us to a sell-out Southsea crowd. Can you imagine booking someone like that today? Unfortunately, just before Edwin went on our resident DJ had realised that he hadn't replaced the batteries in the radio mic.

"Don't worry" said Mac (he was always very calm) "Dean can go on stage with him and make sure he doesn't trip over the cable" (of the wired mic).

So up I went, on stage with Edwin Star whilst he belted out 'War', 'Twenty Five Miles'.

This was a great experience until, half way through his final song, with the crowd already (quite rightly) whipped up into a frenzy with 'Contact', Edwin invites everyone to join him on stage to help him finish 'H.A.P.P.Y. Radio'. Fortunately, I was a bit taller than Edwin and the young ladies now sharing his stage. So, despite being considerably pushed around I managed to keep the mic lead above all of their heads and a grateful Edwin Starr finished his set.

Mac was also grateful, and I was duly invited to share the traditional after-show Chinese Takeaway in his office, just Edwin Starr, Mac Kuleza and me. Two legends and a young lad from Devon.

Some may say that 'the Northern Managers' were lucky to have this experience and then be able to apply it to the ripe fields of the South whilst have fun doing it. But they had already paid their dues.

The point is that there are no short cuts. if you have read this far, you're probably made of the right stuff to be successful. You're willing to go the extra mile, make a bit more effort, you're open to new ideas, and you can embrace change. If you've come this far with me, why not go a little farther? Sign up for one of my digital packages and I'll be happy to give you the odd bit of direction to avoid the potholes and navigate your way to increased footfall, a successful venue and a secure job.

I'd wish you luck, but we both know that luck doesn't have anything to do with it.

EPILOGUE
A Tale Of Two Towns

A s I finish this book, we're now eight weeks away from the date when nightclubs can, theoretically, open up again as the UK's lockdown restrictions come to an end.

It's never in my mind to be openly critical of how a venue operates, this stuff can be hard, right? Just getting into the right mind set to do this well can be hard enough, especially if you've been battered and bruised by world events like most have in the past twelve months. So, I won't mention names, but I want to share with you some details of two new openings that are about to happen in eight weeks' time...

Both are traditional and large nightclub operations, both are in seaside towns, one is in the North of England, one in the South. They are three-hundred miles apart geographically, but a million miles apart in strategy and experience.

One is being opened by the 'great' operators that I know and have worked with for years and they're using the formula that I've highlighted in this book. Literally every trick in this book.

The other is being opened by 'enthusiastic amateurs' who have carried out a great restoration on a wonderful old venue steeped in history and it's their dream.

In the North they have been hard at marketing for months. Networking, selling booths and packages for the opening night (now sold out) and doing all of the steps in Part Three of this book. Their new website has really impressed me, it even shows diagrams of the booth areas available in the VIP section, they've left no stone unturned.

In the South their website holding page says, "website nearly live".

In the North they are opening on a Monday which is the first possible date eight weeks from now – this has been advertised for twelve weeks already.

In the South they haven't decided yet what date they will open, but they're certain that when they do it will be *really busy*.

So, answer one question for me...

If you had to buy shares in one of these businesses, which one would you choose?

ABOUT THE AUTHOR

—————— ◆◆◆ ——————

D ean Sanders has worked in and around the hospitality industry for almost thirty-four years.

In the early days as a member of staff & then as a management trainee for Rank Leisure at the age of 21. Fast forward 4 years & 6 venues to when I joined Luminar Leisure, in the early days, as one of its youngest General Managers. Later a brief 2 years as a bar owner saw him make more than a few mistakes before re-joining Luminar PLC in its hay day.

A move to a large Pub chain followed and then an internal promotion to National Marketing Manager with specific responsibility for re-launches & a wider remit over 55 town centre sites. Next, he was a partner and the Marketing Director of a print company with a digital marketing arm – Footfall Direct, specialising in the hospitality sector. Moving forward another 6 years, Dean left Footfall Direct in November 2019 and set up his own digital marketing company aimed at driving footfall into the hospitality sector.

Printed in Great Britain
by Amazon

81463848R00072